# Sloth

## JOKES & FUN FACTS

For every kid brave enough to think outside the box.

**LITTLE DUMPLING PRESS**
© 2021 ALL RIGHTS RESERVED

All rights reserved. No part of this publication may be reproduced, distributed, or transmitted in any form or by any means, including photocopying, recording, or other electronic or mechanical methods, without the prior written permission of the publisher, except in the case of brief quotations embodied in critical reviews and certain other noncommercial uses permitted by copyright law.

Why are sloths the most social animals?

**They always want to hang out.**

What do you call intelligent sloths?

**Slo-mo sapien.**

What did the sloth say to his friend who was going through a hard time?

**Just hang in there.**

# FUN SLOTH FACT

October 20 is International Sloth Day, a day to honor the slow-moving, tree-dwelling, and leaf-eating mammals.

Why did the sloth get fired from his job?

**He would only do the BEAR minimum.**

Why didn't the sloth go extinct?

It didn't plan on going anywhere.

# FUN SLOTH FACT

Sloths live in the tropical forests of Central and South America, sleeping up to 20 hours a day.

What do you get when you cross a cat and a sloth?

**A slow leopard.**

What do you call it when a sloth eats a second plate of food?

**Slothy seconds.**

What do sloths throw in winter?

**Slowballs.**

# FUN SLOTH FACT

Sloths are solitary and arboreal (tree dwellers) mammals. Although they spend most of their time in the trees, sloths are surprisingly good swimmers. In fact, they are faster in water than on land.

Why do sloths never kiss on the first date?

**They take it slow.**

What does the sloth journalist read every morning when he gets to work?

**A snooze paper.**

What do you call a sloth that barely moves a muscle?

**A slow-off.**

# FUN SLOTH FACT

There are two different types of sloths, two-toed and three-toed.

# FUN SLOTH FACT

Six sloth species exist:
- Pygmy three-toed sloth (Bradypus pygmaeus)
- Maned sloth (Bradypus torquatus)
- Pale-throated sloth (Bradypus tridactylus)
- Brown-throated sloth (Bradypus variegatus)
- Linnaeus's two-toed sloth (Choloepus didactylus)
- Hoffman's two-toed sloth (Choloepus hoffmanni)

What's a sloth's favorite song?

**Don't Hurry, Be Happy.**

Why did the sloth cross the road?

Nobody knows, he's still trying.

Where did the sloth couple first meet?

**At the sloth ball.**

What did the sloth tell his wife on their fifth anniversary?

I'm so glad you're by my side. I love you sloth much.

# FUN SLOTH FACT

The sloth is the world's slowest mammal. They can be 2 to 2.5 feet long and, depending on the species, weigh from 8 to 17 pounds.

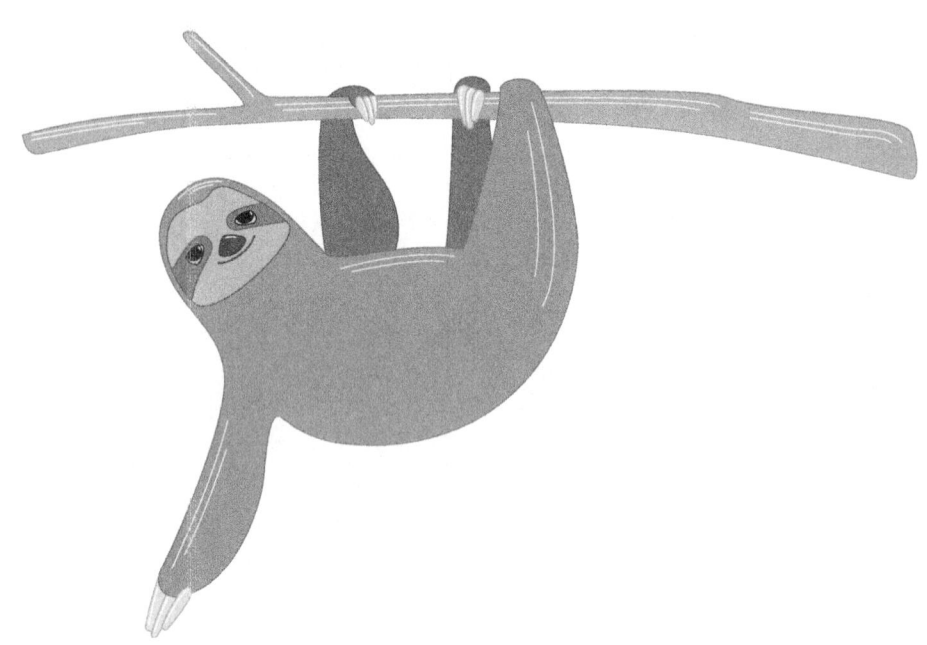

What did the waiter say when the sloth took a deep breath in the middle of giving his order?

**Why such a long paws?**

Why was the sloth giving a lecture about existentialism to his niece?

**He was feeling philoslothical.**

What did they start calling the sloth, who played Othello, when he took so much time to recite his lines?

**They started calling him 'Slowthello'.**

# FUN SLOTH FACT

Sloths are three times stronger than humans.

What do you get when you cross a sloth and a Scottish rock band?

**Slow Patrol.**

How did the sloth introduced his wife to his friends?

**He said, "Hello everyone, as you may know, this is my significant sloth-er."**

Why don't sloths look at their watches to tell the time?

**They find it very time-consuming.**

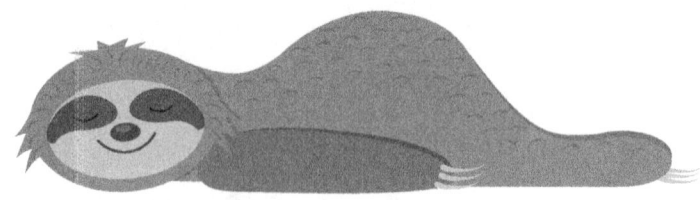

# FUN SLOTH FACT

Sloths can almost turn their heads all the way around to 270 degrees.

When the sloth went to Hogwarts, which House did the Sorting Hat put him in?

**The Slotherin House.**

What is a sloth's favorite activity during wintertime?

**They love to make slow angels.**

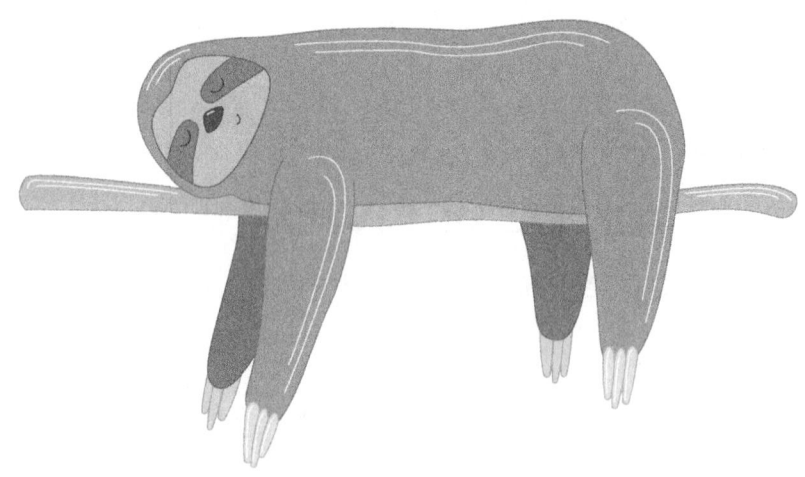

What did they call the old slot machines in the casino?

They worked so slowly that many of the visitors and players called them the sloth machines.

# FUN SLOTH FACT

Sloths have very bad eyesight and are colorblind. Luckily, sloths compensate for their poor vision by having a keen sense of smell and great spatial memory.

What does a sloth order at Starbucks?

**A sloffee**

What did the sloth say to the tree branch?

I'm hooked on you.

Printed in Great Britain
by Amazon